O.K.A.Y

Overseas Korean Artists Yearbook

Volume 1

OKAY Volume 1

Published in Seoul, Korea by JinsolBooks
Publishing Company 2001
star~kim & onegook PROJECT, Seoul Korea

Copyright (c) Mihee N. Lemoine
ISBN 89-86581-60-4 93000
Coordinators: Mihee-Nathalie Lemoine & Kate Hers

Design Coordination: star~kim
Production & Distribution: onegook
Publisher: star~kim & onegook PROJECT
Korean Coordination: Park Young-Sook
Printing Coordination: Park Jin-Deok (JinsolBooks)
Editing Support: Eleanor Soo-Ah Hyun & Matthew
Dolbow
First Draft Layout: Kim Dalros
First Published 2001 - This edition 2001
(c) 2001 star~kim & onegook PROJECT

Contact:
Mihee N. Lemoine
c/o star~kim & onegook PROJECT
K. P.O. Box 1964 Seoul 110-619, Korea
$ 20.00 + $ 5.00 (S & H) per issue
25,000 Won + 4,000 Won (S & H) per issue

Purchase By Mail:
K. P.O. Box 1964, Seoul 110-619, Korea
Purchase By Email:
okaybook@hotmail.com

Please send all correspondence, donations,
and subscriptions to the address above.

2

contents

3

context

Korea has a unique Diaspora. The oldest Korean Diasporic communities are in Japan, China, and Russia. The Korean Diaspora in America began in the 19th century. It expanded to Europe and Australia after World War II. Some 5.3 million Koreans live abroad in 14 different countries. Since 1953, more than 200,000 Koreans have been adopted overseas. Recently Korean people have shown an interest in establishing cultural programs and foundations in and out of the country, in order to benefit from an international recognition of 5,000 years of Korean culture.

At the forefront of this movement have been Korean artists who have studied and worked overseas. International students (Yu-haksaeng) represent the privileged few who are able to afford the high cost of tuition, find the academic contacts that help them get scholarships, or have the political pull to study abroad. Overseas students have had a strong influence on the domestic Korean art scene.

Compared to the Yu-haksaeng, non-native, non-Korean born, non-Korean citizen, non-Korean cultured Korean have limited access to the domestic Korean art community.

Culture shock, language barrier, identity issues, and discrimination hinder the entry of Gyopos, Dongpos, & Adoptees to break into the Korean art world. In addition, the somewhat fixed system of how to climb the ladder of success in art, (for example: going to an acclaimed school to meet the necessary contacts, studying with a famous instructor/artist, or becoming a professor at a University), makes it even more difficult for a Korean living overseas to develop their career in Korea.

In the fall of 1999, there was an open call for submissions. Additionally, about 150 artists were personally invited to participate in this project. Of those contacted, a third expressed interest. Those chosen provided information, both about their work and themselves, for the publication of this book.

The OKAY Book was developed to celebrate the new millennium, motivate young artists, and open a platform for those Koreans abroad to show their work and advance their careers.

introduction

star~kim & onegook PROJECT is proud to announce the publication of the OKAY Book Volume 1, a comprehensive guide of the works of young, emerging overseas Korean artists. Since the beginning of the existence of the Korean Diaspora, this is the first initiative to collect, document, and distribute the works of some 44 artists and groups working in the various art and media fields. It presents an overview of the Korean Diaspora art scene, as well as promotes and builds a strong network and pride of Korean-ness in the global village (Segyewha).

We hope, through this effort, to bring a relationship of exchange with our home countries and our "homeland." We have accepted submissions from artists who are making ORIGINAL WORK, not interpretive (i.e. a musician who plays a piece written by a different artist, or a dancer that follows the movements of a piece choreographed by someone else. Performing artists such as actor(s), dancer(s) and musician(s) were NOT eligible to apply unless they create and perform their own work). We have gathered artists of Korean heritage between the ages of 20-40 years old from all over the world. Although due to communication difficulties, sadly we were not able to receive submissions from any Korean Japanese or Korean Chinese.

star~kim & onegook PROJECT believe that this project can recognize young emerging artists and groups of artists who have been productive in their countries of emigration and elsewhere. These artists of Korean ethnicity have been developing an art, overseas and/or in their "motherland," which deserves to be noticed and recognized.

Upon seeing a Bordas Edition "Le Dictionnaire de la Peinture Moderne," and similar books published in English, such as "The Art Book," we asked ourselves why not create one based on the history of the Korean Art Diaspora? We represent a new generation of artists to succeed the already well known overseas Korean artists, Paik Nam June and Theresa Hak Kyung Cha, the founding Godfather and Godmother to the artistic expression of cultural Diaspora, displacement, and identity.

star~kim & onegook PROJECT will continue to produce the works of active emerging, young artist. In celebration of collaboration between Korea and Japan in the 2002 World Cup Series, we will commence with a new project emphasizing works of artists represented from each country.

5

6

Birthplace & year: NYC, 1976
Graduated from Columbia University with a B.A.
in Art History. Worked in the Departments of
Asian Art and European Paintings at the
Metropolitan Museum of Art, New York.
Received a Fulbright Scholarship to Korea in
1999 to research Korean paintings of the
Choson dynasty. While in Seoul, interned at the
National Museum of Korea, Seoul and Ewha
Woman's University Museum. Will be attending
graduate school in Fall 2001 to research Korean
and Chinese ceramics.

by Eleanor Soo-ah HYUN

foreword

OKAY Book Vol. 1 is an important vehicle for emerging artists of Korean ethnicity. Overseas Korean artists often find themselves marginalized both in their home countries, where they are part of the ethnic minority, and when they return to Korea, due to their unfamiliarity with the country and culture. As a result of being pushed to the periphery, it is difficult to find a platform to express their art, and ultimately their voice. Additionally, when given a stage to exhibit the art, it is under specific conditions in order to categorize the artist. OKAY not only provides an opportunity to exhibit art, but is also, perhaps more importantly, a place free of preconceptions.

While ethnic Koreans find themselves generalized and expected to play certain roles within society, OKAY offers a glimpse into the diversity within the Korean Diaspora. The artists have different backgrounds, some have had a lot of contact throughout their lives with Korea and the culture and others have had little or no experience with it. There is no single theme that runs through all the art presented in this volume. Although most of the artists work within the dialogue of identity, there are many facets of identity being explored. Susan Sponsler, Zoli Kim Hall, Tammy Tolle, Leah Sieck, Me-K Ahn, Meaghan Dunn, and Kevin Kahiler, all Korean adoptees, make adoption the subject of their works. Contrastingly, Michou Amelynck, Vincent Sung, J. Maya Weimer, Charlotte Kim Boed, Yun Sook Kim Navarre, Kate Hers, Jung, and Mihee-Nathalie Lemoine, also Korean adoptees, do not focus on adoption, but center more broadly on the Asian experience. Cecilia H. Lee, Lola Lee, Stephanie Han, Raymond Hahn, Jiwon Chun, and JeeYun Ha are Korean-Americans and address the issues of categorization, both in their minority and gender status. The works of Kimberly Kaye Nam-Il Dalros, Minjung Kim, Hyuna Park, Ji-Young Oh, Jill M. Pfenning, Meejah I-Ley, Song Huff, and Jean Jung are more abstract and do not express specific subject matter.

OKAY reflects a new generation of overseas Korean artists, who, in an age of globalization and economic prosperity, have more opportunities to create a discourse within the Korean Diaspora. However, this should only be the beginning in developing a network and forum to exchange ideas. The majority of the artists in this volume come from the United States and there are many countries with ethnic Koreans that are not represented, i.e. Japan, Australia, Argentina, and etc. Thus, it is important that this book is considered "volume 1," allowing for subsequent volumes to expand the discourse and network.

OKAY Book Vol. 1 is a breakthrough book because it provides a platform *for* overseas Korean artists, individuals who have been long been unheard, *by* overseas Korean artists.

7

lexical

Dongpo
Brothers: brethren: fellow countrymen;
one's countrymen; compatriots; fellow creature

Gyopo
A Korean resident (national) abroad;
a Korean residing abroad; overseas Koreans

1.5 / ilchumo
Born in Korea, emigrated as a child

2nd generation
Born overseas from Korean parents

Ibyang
Adoptee/adoption

Haewae Ibyang
Overseas adoptee

Ibyang-A
Adopted child

Ibyang-In
Adult adoptee

Me-K AHN
Michou AMELYNCK
Charlotte Kim BOED
Jiwon CHUN
Kimberly Kaye Nam-Il DALROS
Meaghan DUNN & Kevin KAHILER
JeeYun HA
Raymond HAHN
Zoli Kim HALL
Stephanie HAN
Kate HERS
Song HUFF
Meejah I-LEY
JUNG
Jean JUNG
Minjung KIM
Cecilia H. LEE
Lela LEE
Mihee-Nathalie LEMOINE
Yun Sook Kim NAVARRE
Ji-Young OH
Hyuna PARK
Jill M. PFENNING
Leah SIECK
Susan SPONSLER
Vincent SUNG
Tammy TOLLE
J. Maya WEIMER

9

ahn ME-K

living in halftones, 1994
Experimental short
9 min.

Birthplace & year: Incheon, 1968
Resides in Minneapolis; short films screened
internationally; stories published nationally;
received grants for film and literary production.
Currently adapting a novel-in-progress into a
feature film and developing a docu-drama.

Statement

When I returned to Korea in the fall of 1992, I
felt a certain amount of detachment, alienation
from my birthplace. It mirrored, oddly enough,
my situation in the States since 1970, the year I
was adopted. I half expected that once I was
back in Korea, my biological connection would
be reactivated, that I would be able to tap into
the far reaches of my psyche and rediscover
what it "really" meant to be Korean. Instead, I
felt estranged, unwelcomed, like the outcast I
became when I was abandoned.

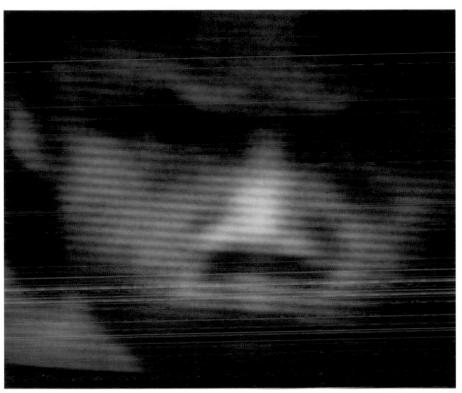

living in halftones, 1994

ahn ME-K

undertow, 1997
Experimental short
18 min.

12

Description

living in half tones is a metaphorical (re)construction of my developing Korean identity. Through recently captured visual imagery, simulated archival footage and text, it explores my experience of returning to Korea for the first time to search for fragments of my past. It serves as the visual linguistic for the confusion, pain and struggle that such a search entails.

undertow is a meditative short video-film that explores the impact of family and cultural loss on one's body consciousness and sexuality. It juxtaposes one woman's reconstructed search for her birth mother with the attempt to connect mind and body. Through the multilayered incorporation of text, dramatic and documentary footage, voice over and body movement, the internal challenges of crawling back into a murky past are revealed.

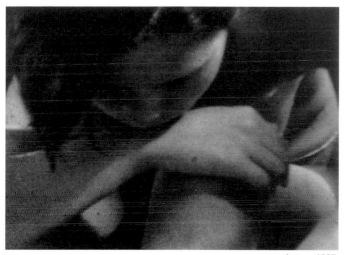

undertow, 1997

13

Here and Near, 1996
Make-up

Statement

I am attracted to traditional make-up in general
and fabric/patchwork, but especially of Asian
origins because of the beauty, the colors, the
preciseness and the patterns. The traditional
side, moving as it is, gives a sense of
importance to keep something alive for decades
and centuries.

14

Birthplace & year: Seoul, 1969
Studied dance and stage make up at the Finotto
Professional Make-up School.
Currently lives and works in Brussels as a free-
lance make up artist and AD modeling.

Here and Near, 1996

Le Chemin de l'Anabiose, 2000
(The Way of Rebirth)
Craftwork
30 x 22 cm / 12 x 8.5 in.

Description

This patchwork represents a stage of my
search for identity. The choice of naive style is
cheerful and light and explores childlike
freedom.

16

Le Chemin de l'Anabiose, 2000

Moods of Silver, 1998
Color photo
20 x 21 cm / 8 x 8.3 in.

Statement

In our human existentialism, I wish to see the common compounding dependence of the past years connections, between things, people, and events.

Birthplace & year: Pusan, 1968
Adopted in 1970 to Denmark. In 1996 returned to Korea for the first time and met her biological parents. Has since visited Korea several times, and studied Korean at Kyung-Hee University in Seoul.
Currently lives in Copenhagen, Denmark

Series print from Moods of Silver, 1998

Identities, 2000
(Sara, Teen, Daniel, Charlotte)
Computer enhanced images
40.5 x 15 cm / 16 x 12 in.

Description

The series of pictures *Identities*, I try through
the media of photographic settings, to work with
and familiarize with Asiatic peoples,
incorporating identities. I attempt to create
psychological layers of moods, and to explore
and promote existential occurrence. I search
for the common of people's moments, through
different kind of mirrors and archetypes.

20

Sara, 2000

Teen, 2000

Daniel, 2000

Charlotte, 2000

chun JIWON

Our Home, 2001, Chicago
152.5 x 152.5 x 213.5 cm / 5 x 5 x 8 ft
500 sponges
Each sponge 12.5 x 20.5 x 5 cm / 5 x 8 x 2 in.

Statement

The natural cycle and circulation is a motion and movement that is embetted in our everyday lives. The use of the domestic object best represents the stage at which I have found myself in the familiar cycle of life.

22

Birthplace & year: Po-Hang, 1977
Grew up in the Bay Area, Nothern California.
Graduated from School of the Art Institute a of Chicago with a BFA.

23

Our Home, 2001

Rubbing, 1999, Chicago
Performance
122 x 213.5 cm / 4 x 7 ft
20-30 min.

Blue, Red, Yellow sponge, 1999
Paper
5 x 12.5 x 25.5 cm / 2 x 5 x 10 in.

24

Description

I started in a corner like one would when cleaning a space. Words appeared on the paper the more I rubbed the surface of the paper in a repetitive motion. This piece touches on the erasing and remembering memories, revealing and unrevealing the past, and scrubbing and rubbing to find history.

Our Home project was something I taught high school students last semester. Assignment: Generate ideas on the concept of "home" to create relationship between words with visual art on sponges to construct a house. Each student made a list of twenty words to define "home" and wrote papers to further understand their notion of what a "home" means to them. "Home" can mean a place where one feels safe, comfort, and respect. Home could be your community, neighborhood, family, friends, school or work place. Students came together to share and express their individual experiences and stories to build a home.

Rubbing, 1999

Blue Sponge, 1999

Balance, 1998
Charcoal & Conte crayon
30.5 cm x 20 cm / 12 x 8 in.

Statement

As I realize more, the creative process helps
me along the journey to discover peace...with
life and myself.

Birthplace & year: Namwon, 1971
Has been active with local organizations that
benefit the adopted Korean and art communities
in the Twin Cities. Has worked in the art
direction and graphic design field for over six
years. Within the past 2 years, freelanced with
various newspapers, city magazines,
businesses, and organizations in the Twin Cities
area.

Balance, 1998

Landscape, 1997
Charcoal & Conte crayon
23 x 30.5 cm / 9 x 12 in.

Description

Finger charcoal…A little over three years ago, I
was reacquainted with the charcoal medium
and found myself lost with joy in the forms that
were created on paper. With the different types
of charcoal and white Conte crayon, I would
start with a point, line and/or streak and then
followed my fingers and palms wherever they
traveled on the paper. It was kind of like finger
painting, like a kid in second grade...

28

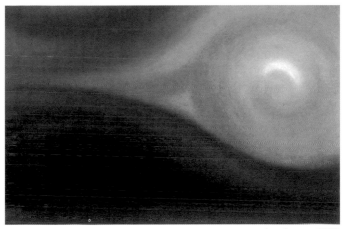

Landscape, 1997

dunn MEAGHAN & kahiler KEVIN

Don't be Latte, 2000
Black & white ink on paper
43 x 28 cm / 17 x 11 in.

Statement

Kitty Bobo is a cat adopted by dogs and at times we've explored adoptee issues in our artwork with this device. But there's a lot of fun to be had in stories that have nothing to do with adoption. This is one of them, an Archie-esque two page comic.

Birthplace & year: Hong'do,1972 / Pusan, 1973
Dunn and Kahiler currently work in the animation industry and live in Los Angeles with their two cats.

Don't be Latte, 2000

Don't be Latte, 2000
Black & white ink on paper
43 x 28 cm / 17 x 11 in.

Description

2 page comic. Penciling by Kahiler. Lettering
and inking by Dunn.

32

Don't be Latte, 2000

Falling, 2000
Oil on wood
45 x 37 cm / 17.5 x 14.5 in.

Statement

My work has definitive sensual/sexual elements
in texture, color, Image, or subject matter. The
personal and the political /social is completely
intertwined and this is what I hope is reflected in
my art. Using much of the color red: a loaded
color, seductive and appealing to the eye, I
associate blood, hot, passion, madness, joy,
good luck (east), whore (west), celebration,
spicy, erotic, stop, burning (desire), and shame.

34

Birthplace & year: Pusan, 1976
Graduated from Parson's School of Design with
a BFA. Shown her work in Detroit, MI, El Paso,
TX, and NY. Has shown at J. Rainey Gallery in
Detroit, MI. Taught art in elementary schools
and participated in teaching and coordinating a
summer arts program for children in Detroit.
Currently resides in Seoul.

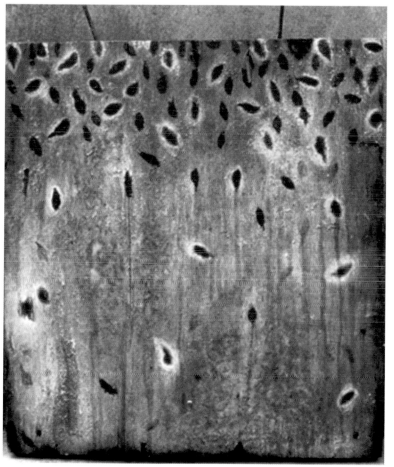

Falling, 2000

Burning Bush, 1998
Installation, wood, red pepper, ceramic
300 x 200 cm / 9.8 ft x 5.7 ft

Shouldn't Touch, 1998
Oil on wood
200 x 300 cm / 5.7 x 9.8 ft

36

Description

The work is sensual through texture, color,
image, or subject matter (the personal to the
political). The work comprises much more than
just these elements, yet they are fundamental
nonetheless. The color red emerges often,
while many pieces are exclusively red: red
paint, crushed red pepper, red hots, red velvet,
and red thread. The pieces are made from
wood of many forms, mainly branches. There
is beauty in the aging and disintegration of
objects particularly wood and metal. There are
many associations with the color red, especially
'hotness'. Temperature hot, hot- tempered,
spicy hot, hot with desire, hot with shame.
Trees are a symbol of life; women produce life;
lives can be whole, broken, or shattered.

Burning Bush, 1998

Shouldn't Touch, 1998

hahn RAYMOND

The ID Line, 1999
Computer manipulated image
Dimension variable

Statement

My work involves examining some of the
relationships that exist between geography and
culture in an Asian American frame of context.
I attempt to analyze the extent of identification a
person may have with their ethnic background
and the circumstances that promote or preclude
this.

38

Birthplace & year: Los Angeles, 1967
A 2nd generation Korean-American
photographer who lives in Los Angeles,
California and Seoul, Korea. Likes drinking
coffee late at night while watching Hong Kong
movies.

At 40,000 feet, is this the neutral territory I seek?

The ID Line, 1999

hahn RAYMOND

Crossing My Own Pacific Ocean, 1999
Computer manipulated image
Dimension variable

40

Description

In the image *The ID Line*, I wanted to propose that the feeling of home is a state of mind subject to the vagaries of time and experience. We think of a geographic map as a permanent arrangement of nature of politics but these change over time. The idea of home is transitory and malleable like everything else.

The image, *Crossing my Own Pacific Ocean*, refers to the Pacific Ocean as a neutral space, totally oblivious to your ports of arrival and departure. When traveling by airplane at high altitude there is the added element of not being restricted to land, with the consequence of "jumping" over all your problems, fears, hopes and other concerns that affected passengers wherever they were or wherever they're headed.

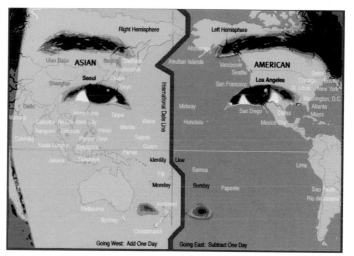

Crossing My Own Pacific Ocean, 1999

hall ZOLI KIM

For Omoni, 2000
Poem
Published in Asian Pacific American Journal,
V.8 Nr. 2 / V.9 / Nr. 1 Summer/Spring 2000

42

Birthplace & year: Korea, 1970
Writer and artist living in Minneapolis. Received
a 1999 Jerome Foundation Travel/Study Grant
and showcased her work at the 2000 KAAN
conference. Published in several local and
national publications, including The Asian
American Renaissance Journal: Sexual
Orientations, and Seeds from a Silent Tree; An
Anthology By Korean Adoptees. Recent
publications include the Asian Pacific American
Journal and Drumvoices Revue.
Currently editing her chapbook entitled Portrait
of an Orphan's Memoryscape.

Statement

Adopted at the age of three by an American
couple. She grew up in Dallas, TX and
Minneapolis, MN and surrounding suburbs.
Zoli's art explores, challenges, and meditates
on her multiple identities as a Korean American
adoptee, citizen, orphan immigrant, artist and
woman. Through the traditions of poetry and
visual art, she hopes to continue exploring the
invisible text beneath the grammar of
complacent aesthetics as well as the silences of
history.

"The very term orphan reflects the uniqueness
of a solitary, insighful state. The alchemists
originally used the word to name a unique gem
once found in the emperor's crown, similiar to
the philosopher's stone, considered both
worthless and priceless, despised by fools but
loved by the wise. Even then, it was believed
that orphans held special knowledge and
acquired and insight others had not attained."
- Hope Edleman, "Motherless Daughter's; The
legacy of Loss."

For Omoni *

All day I have felt you moving south inside of me
Shadows of your legs, brush across my arms

Your sad thoughts waver through my breath
As I watch raindrops swim drunkenly down

The glass ponds of windows.
How do we grieve for what we can't remember?

I am a veteran of your heartbeat as I sit in this chair.
I have not left you yet, sound of afternoon rain

Light staccato entering the song
Where there is no childhood.

In a city, that comes from a past, that can never be a city again
Where I watched the days of your hunger

And the water that you drank to fill up the hours
Waiting for the aura of fullness to fill you back

To my crying mouth
Your grasp, I felt fading from my life

Losing me to the air, as I fell through that spiral of panic
Five feet of height, to the floor.
*

This wet season dampens the rooms of the body
Mold swells the channels of my fingertips
Spores of memory not quite solid
Make me sneeze with surrender

*

I dream of your body always
I love to watch the smoky curve of your spine,

Lift and then rise up, a stairway leading to the
bottom of your hair, the blackest velvet
Where my hand reaches out and rests

Soft, in that hollow of space,
When I dream your body back to me

I hear the dawn of sorrow in a morning dove's song
The lilies in the field still white in the last hour of dark,

43

A hand turning the leaf of the page
In the story I know you would keep, if I told it to
you again

In a kingdom where an orphan always eats first,
Inside the cave of the forest where she was found
asleep

Underneath the sky
Where the stars are all echoes of her lives that
were lost and then found.

                    * Korean word for mother

hall ZOLI KIM

For Omoni; part II, 2000
Poem
Published in The Journal of The Asian
American Renaissance, Spirits, Myths, and
Dreams: Stories in Transit V.4 Summer 2000

Description

Her work touches on transracial parent child
relations, the nuances of memory, language,
sexuality, beauty, and power in the context of
her American experience. She utilizes both
descriptive and broken narratives to illustrate
and deconstruct the global theme and myths of
each specific poem and series of art works.

44

For Omoni; part II

If I search for you through the center of absence,
I can see how I barely remember your face before this

So I will begin again with the Korean monks always there,
In the back of my three old memory, returning me
To the empty room of the house that night, on
December 23rd, 1973,
    Something inside the heart stops here.

If you looked out beyond the window this evening
You would see the sun splashing a late angle
Of summer light against brick building,
Inside the studio, it is cool as the ancient air conditioner
Hums along side the harmonica's melody rising from the radio,
    It is eight twenty seven in the evening.

I am still motioning flesh to paper and the paper
Toward the undulant detail in which memories and
histories survive.
In earlier moments, I remembered you
As the language of leaves I had dreamed
    After the monks had gone and there was no one
left to watch.

Once when I awakened inside the darkness of
my first apartment,
I heard a woman's voice sweep against me like wind,
The question that she delivered;
    Who will be there to tell her whhat her
memory has lost?
Lingered thick as smoke at the edge of my bed
My heart panicked for daylight as I raced to
open the fog kissed windows.

Long ago, I feared the absence of you first,
And I looked for you everywhere, with a longing I
never felt for anyone else,
    I know the orphan of my past comes from this,

I have loved you again,
And now the unkempt hour of this sorrow, I give to you
As ghst's dream our way back
These yongson* clouds closing over the city
Without lightning maps, repeating so fast
As I wait for thunder to break
I will not mistake it for departure.

*Korean word for the ghost of a person who
traveled far from home and died a stranger.

45

han STEPHANIE

Pale Yellow Moon, 1995
L.A. (Lovers Anonymous) Lala Press
P.38

Statement

Maternal family (Han) came nearly 100 years
ago to Hawaii from Korea; paternal family (Yoo)
is from Seoul, Korea. Her recent work (fiction
and nonfiction/academic) has addressed
feminism, sexuality, identity, and nation.

Description

Poetry/prose book L.A. (Lovers Anonymous)
takes a contemporary look at sex and romance
in Los Angeles.

46

Birthplace & year: St. Louis, MO, 1964
Attended Phillips Academy Andover; Barnard
College/Columbia University; U.C. Santa
Barbara (BA); San Francisco State University
(MA). Recipient of two L.A. Department of
Cultural Affairs Grants for Writing, Corwin
Screenwriting Award and a PEN West Emerging
Voices Fellowship. Completing a collection of
short stories about Korean/Korean diaspora
women and is writing a pansori play for pansori
artist Chan Park, scheduled for 2003
performance at University of Hawaii. Married to
British writer Stephen Aldred.

Pale Yellow Moon

I am your pale yellow moon,
against the night of sighs and moans.

I am your shadowed lover
kissing the tender skin.

I am your dark confession
of twisted words.

Yield to me your desires
in the abyss of sordid dares.

Return to me the hope
of desperate writhing flesh.

Cry to me your wish
of lost will and gathered strength

As time weaves
its helix clock

as lover weep
and leave

as stars fall
and rise;

you wonder
if I
hidden by day
emerging at dusk-

will forever be
splendid and ripe?

Yes, I am full of the seasons!

Bountiful and plenty
I can never empty.

Lover you have no boundaries
Reach for me besides you-

I am your pale yellow moon.

47

The Kill Is Desire, 1995
L.A. (Lovers Anonymous) Lala Press
P. 77

48

The Kill Is Desire

Ravaged with lustful eyes
and groping hands she pouts and sucks
Watch him, television begging with murmurs
and sweet talk cheapened with drunken
scent of money and age.
She takes and opens as they sweat and mount
artfully turning her head
gazing up with half closed
lids and smeared mascara.

Woman, whore, friend
all alone in the same to Him.
He is all
Dark/fair skin, old/young eyes
rich/destitute in age or vision.
She invents accordingly.
Girl, Nymph, Child
Dominant/Compliant
Woman of the world
East or West, China Doll, Geisha, Island Girl
Intellect, Bunny, Toy, Owner or Pet.

What's he want?
She gives it
shark smiles and hair swinging.
Watch her smirk
for she knows the trade.
Skin pale and smooth
eyes almond dark with lascivious intent
lips stung with the red paint.

Raging she demands and they comply.
She screws on lids of compassion
grabbing fingers breaking bones
carefully running tiny pads and pointed toes
down a spine
kneading flesh
and spinning sordid webs
kissing and crawling between
legs contorted with pleasure
edged with razor blades and steel.
Sixty-nine, up, down, on top or bottom,
choke it, suck it, devour my love -
do it all styles. Watch them rock.
Hey Mister, Baby, Lover, Boyfriend
Whatever-your-name-is,
let me give it to you good.
Wild groaning pants of unstoppable fury
shaking the wave thunders.
He rides it.
Rollercoaster hang on.
The night begins.

Momentary meeting
blissful hell
they fling and thrust
beads of sweat dropping from bodies
like hot shower movies.
She eats him for breakfast.
In her mouth he is nothing.
Disdain? Passion pleasure?
So you care my darling boy?
Shove it, exploding grasps and moans
watch as he crawls to her.

Inside her darkness swallows
and they are locked as the pulse
screams for release
Who gives and who takes?
Day break: Artifice and Illusion
Femme Fatale or Playmate
Thing of Men and Power of Skin
Don't you like it raw?
Isn't that what you wanted?

Angry in blue hot flashes
She leaves with the sour taste of liquid and sweat.
Simple disheveled
with rumpled clothes she turns over
a quick kiss? Or a slap?
The scorn begins.
He sleeps - a baby by day.
Anger erupting pathos silenced
remembrance milked up to blow out.
She is a hunter craving blood
returning with machete strong and guns of
vicious sounds.
Spitting, digging her heel into crying flesh.
Watch him shriek and cower.
Poor Man.
Stupid Beast.
Don't you like it that way?
Pay now
It's the wake up call
Ah-the Kill is desire

49

hers KATE

My Country 'Tis of Thee, 2001, Seoul
Korean flag, kimchi, 4 hospital surgeons
Installation performance
30 min.

Statement

Adopted at the age of 6 months old by an American couple, Kate grew up in Detroit, Michigan. Since her return to Korea for the first time in 1997, she has been dedicated to an art-making that attempts to reinvent "Korean-ness," while incorporating the influences of her adoption history, her recent explorations in Korean culture, and her Western upbringing. She hopes to raise a consciousness in the Korean race, American people, and Adoptee community that there is not just one way to be an American, a woman, a Korean, or an Adoptee.

50

Birthplace & year: Seoul, 1976
Conceptual performance artist. Graduated from the School of the Art Institute of Chicago with a BFA in Time Arts (film, video, performance, sound). Received a Finalist Award Illinois Arts Council and a Fulbright Scholarship to Korea in 2000. Awarded a Blakemore Foundation Language Scholarship in 2001. Taught performance art at Kaywon School of Art & Design in Seoul.

My Country 'Tis of Thee, 2001

Sexy Girlfriend, 2000, Seoul
Performance
25 min.

American Milk, 1997, Chicago/Seoul
Performance
20 min.

Description

Her works are about a process of art-making as
well as performing a "finished" gesture in front
of an audience and receiving a response. It is
not only about expressing an identity as a
Korean American, who happens to be adopted
and who happens to be a woman, but also
discovering the meanings of identities within a
precise context. Each action is created
specifically for the country in which it is shown,
with a deep interest in the culture and race of
the viewers.

52

Sexy Girlfriend, 2000

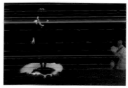

American Milk, 1997

Popular, 1997-1999
Pen on paper
19 x 11.5 cm / 7.5 x 4.5 in.

Will Power, 1997-1999
Pen and color ink on paper
19 x 11.5 cm / 7.5 x 4.5 in.

Statement

I have enjoyed painting and drawing and many
other art forms for 10 years. There has always
been a running theme of reflection upon people
and our interactions and inner thoughts. I take
pleasure from the ironies, the sarcasm, and the
outright ridiculous or absurdity of our human
condition. Finding sweet in the bitter and silent
humor in the disturbed, my art seeks to produce
an attractively awkward commentary.

54

Birthplace & year: Incheon, 1975
Raised in Bethesda, MD outside of Washington
DC. Studied and graduated International
Bachelaureate of Art, Lesin, Switzerland and
traveled extensively. A graduate of SUNY New
Paltz College, BFA Painting. Attended Empire
State College Studio Program in New York City.
Currently resides in Los Angeles, California.

one man's philosophy

Popular, 1997-1999

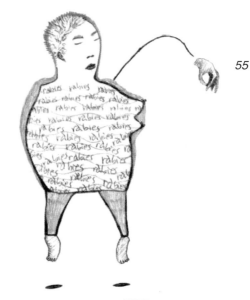

55

Will Power, 1997-1999

Untitled, 1997-1999
Pen on paper
19 x 11.5 cm / 7.5 x 4.5 in.

Asian Baby, 1997-1999
Pen on paper
19 x 11.5 cm / 7.5 x 4.5 in.

Description

These are a handful from a compilation of
drawings. Silly, awkward, translations of
intimate reflections often intended to portray
sarcasm and truth. Sexuality or just sexual?
Many drawings have a sexual tension that is a
reoccurring theme in daily life. These drawings
are a result of the tidbits of everyday life and
philosophical daydreams.

56

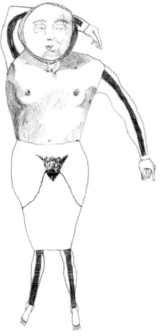

Untitled, 1997-1999

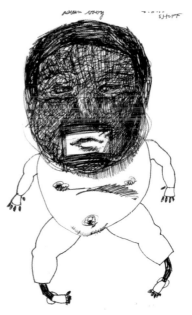

57

Asian Baby, 1997-1999

i-ley MEEJAH painting

war, 1999
Acrylic
51 x 63.5 cm / 20 x 25 in.

Statement

Moments
Twined by fate
Detached - Forgotten - Dispersed
Evanescent fragments of history
Lingering

My concern lies in the realm of life and death;
conscious and dream-life - weaving together the
little deaths, the coming of ages.
Understanding the nature of our lives and
shadow lives. Time marked by strife, relished in
small favors.

58

Birthplace: Korea
Currently lives and works in Korea.

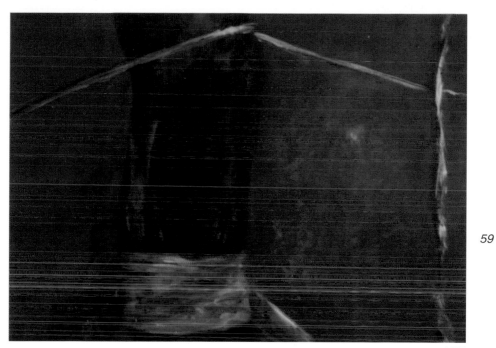

war, 1999

i-ley MEEJAH

stranded, 1999
Acrylic
51 x 63.5 cm / 20 x 25 in.

60

Description

Ties that Bind: My ties to my homeland were
dissolved upon arrival to the New World.
Disassociation was inherent to my
displacement. All sense of ties and bounds and
boundaries rendered useless, I now attempt to
create them. Small, sometimes fragile
connections to the world. Tie myself a place of
my choosing to call home; to persons and
people to call loved. I see ties as associative
forces, at times constraining, at times
comforting. The way in which we relate to
others is often arbitrary - fixed and unplanned.
Trees are both metaphor and manifestation of
life. Seen externally, only a suggestion of
internal conflict. Wrappings and supports hint
at other dramas. New springs, fall - winter -
spring, deep roots and steady foundation. Long
lives initiate sage advice.

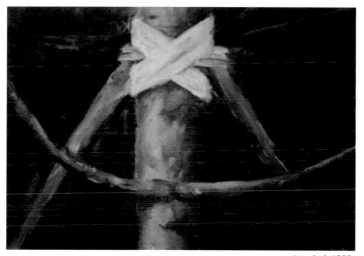

stranded, 1999

jung

Jeune Fille et le Vent (Album 3), 1999
(from The Young Girl and the Wind)
China ink & watercolor ink on paper
44 x 32 cm / 17.5 x 12.5 in.

Statement

The finality of drawings is for him to make a
show through emotions and feelings, with
characters quite present and alive. To tell
stories with images. The drawing is the means
to the end. Even though it is violent and
exotic, all the elements have a purpose in
relationship with the story.

62

Birthplace & year: Seoul ,1965
Adopted by a Belgian family in 1971 with the
name Jung Henin. Studied with a workshop at
Saint Luc of Brussels, and the Academy of the
Art schools of Brussels, Illustration section. Met
Marc Michetz. Illustrated for Spirou and Tintin
magazines. Worked in Hislaire and Darasse
Workshops and illustrated covers of Belgian
Business Magazine. In 1991, published the first
of the four volumes of the Yasuda series, at
Heyode-Lefranc. In 1997, with Martin Ryelandt,
carried out the Young Girl and the Wind, with
the Delcourt editions.

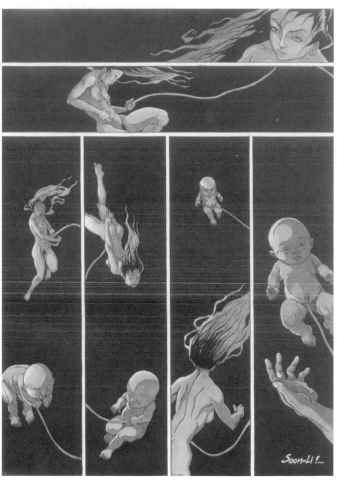

Jeune Fille et le Vent, 1999

Jeune Fille et le Vent (album 3), 1999
(from The Young Girl and the Wind)
Acrylic on paper
30 x 22 cm / 12 x 9 in.

Description

The Asian universe of this series of heroic-fantasy, is a return to its Korean origins, and the fantastic one enables him to reinforce the evocative side of its drawing, in particular for the hero: Wind.

64

E.A. 9/11   APOSTROPHE   JUNG 99

Jeune Fille et le Vent, 1999

jung JEAN

Untitled, 1997, Seoul
Performance
15 min.

Statement

In my performance work I seek to explore and expose new modes of being within different cultural contexts. As a second-generation Korean American woman living in Seoul for the past five years, I am interested in challenging preconceived notions of Asian femininity, moving within and without the complexity of cultural interfaces and the issues that arise from those interfaces, as well as simply navigating the terrain of solo improvisation-based movement performance. I strive to create innovative and liberating expressions on the continuum between stillness and movement.

66

Birthplace & year: Youngstown, OH, 1968
Is an intense improvisation-based movement artist, who is really flexible, too, which comes in handy.
Currently lives and breathes in Seoul, Korea, and performs in order to push the boundaries of her own existence as well as to explore exciting extremes of human interaction.

Untitled, 1997

Untitled, 1997, Seoul
Performance
15 min.

Description

My dance/movement improvisation-based performance encompasses a range of styles and forms. Trained early in ballet and modern techniques and later in postmodern forms including releasing work, Feldenkrais movement therapy and Japanese Butoh, I freely draw from one or more of these disciplines as well as from a self-developed idiosyncratic movement vocabulary. I present meditative, minimalist pieces to silence or other bare sound elements and explore a simple, fairly concrete progression, often challenging notions of timing as well as more dynamic movement performances, often to pop songs, that may disrupt spatial boundaries.

68

Untitled, 1997

kim MINJUNG

Missed Flight, 2000
Poem

Statement

I find resolution to much of the conflict that I
experience in my life through my writing.
Emotional conflict, a need for healing, an
acceptance of affection, and an understanding
of my identity as both Korean and American
come out in my pieces. Most of my writing is
very organic in how it comes to me and
develops. My current projects include an online
humor column for an Asian American web zine
at www.iistix.com and a screenplay which may
or may not ever see the light of day.

70

Birthplace & year: Seoul, 1974
University of Michigan Alumna from the San
Francisco. Has been published in the Detroit
Free Press, Asian American's Women's Journal,
APA Voices, We-Woori Magazine, Mosaics,
Poetry Heaven Quarterly, and several online
publications. Continually working on a growing
anthology of poetry and musings. Any
reference to husbands, spouses, ghosts,
nicotine habits, etc., is used with poetic license
and is now happily single despite anything her
father or grandmother might say.

Missed Flight

I. Silken wet, warm, drops
    soaking the scent
    of Paris nights
    into my skin
    like
    depressions
    of your touch on my arms
    held in a tight, amber
    dream.

II. Tonight
    you cling to me again
    with the memory
    of things that never happened
    Could have but didn't.

iii. What should have been
    still echoes
    in amaretto whispers
    coughed grey
    and pearl by
    paper sparrows above my head.

    What should have been.
    Playful lover memories
    photographic gems of us together
    In this now lonesome bed.
    a lost love

By: Min Jung Kim C: 08/22/00 -
Inspired by the obvious

Restless, 1996
Poem

Brick, 1995
Poem

Description

As always, everything and everyone is a work
in progress. These poems were inspired
particularly by my relationship with my mother
and grandmother.

72

Restless

Nervous cricket, I cannot sleep
Count your thick lashes instead of sheep

Winter blows scrape my thin skin
My breast frostbitten from within

Aching to cling to brandy memories
Trains on rapture, falling to my knees

Whispers of warning, love rests not here
Trains howling laughter, jacklighting deer

Waltzing in dreamland, empty dance book,
Rainbow nightmares mouth torn by a hook,
I lay my head on your wide chest
Close weary eyes, cry to rest

Brick

Coarse
Like my husband fingertips
Scratching the curve of my navel.

How long has this block
Slaved in the sun to turn so red,
and so dusty.

On the roof of our home, I lie down.
His sweat still trickles down my spine.
Choppy seas above me, I see crests of stars
And a solo moon,
Floating gently like the silky slick breast of a whale.

73

Soaring upwards I long to be touched
by something
that does not scrape my skin.

Alone I think.
I breath slowly, wondering about the loving,
Dusty stone beneath my head.

Medicine Balls, 2000
Mixed media
32 x 32 x 32 cm / 12.5 x 12.5 x 12.5 in.

Statement

In my work, I convey different aspects of humanity drawn from my own experiences working, traveling, and from daily interactions. I believe that specifics can lead to the understanding of the general. Thus, I strive to create a dialogue with my artwork which may be specific in detail, but which relates to the human condition as a whole. I see creating as a very personal experience -- first, between the artist and the medium, then, between the viewer and the work. Paradoxically, art is very much about community and activates in a very public realm. In my works I am continually striving to juxtapose the two sides - to have a very intimate dialogue in creating and communicating as well as making my work accessible to the average person.

74

Birthplace & year: Seoul, 1970
Immigrated to the United States in 1977.
Receiving her Bachelors of Art degree in Visual Art at the University of California, San Diego. Spent some time in Mexico discovering printing techniques and learning Spanish. In 1995, spent six months in Korea for cultural research. Collaborated with artist Narciso Arguelles to design a memorial for Cesar E. Chavez, commissioned by the University of Southern California, dedicated in 1998.
Currently resides in Los Angeles.

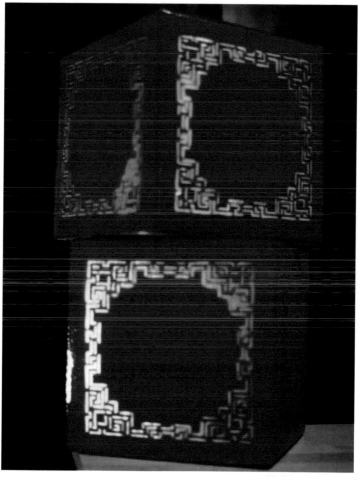

Medicine Balls, 2000

Folktale Frogs, 1997
Paper origami, tape recorder, audio material,
variable dimensions (min. 210 cm / 84 in.
diameter). Audio: approx.1.38MB

Land of Turtles, 1999
Installation, origami & acrylic on canvas
76 cm / 30 in. diameter

76

Description

I work mainly in mixed media and installation
because my art is an all-encompassing
experience. It challenges more than just the
visual senses. This leaves more room for each
person to take away a different meaning from
the work. The medium I choose to work with is
a combination of traditional materials (e.g. paint,
pastel, writing) juxtaposed with found-objects
(e.g. flowers, doorknobs, lipstick) in an attempt
to further blur the already indistinct line between
life and art. My works deal with more visceral
emotions and experiences that dissipate the
boundaries created by culture, language and
social class. I also like to challenges
preconceived notions about women, art,
science, and everything else. By questioning
the status quo, it forces the viewer to confront
widely accepted norms and their own ideas
about them.

Folktale Frogs, 1997

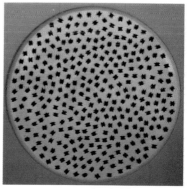

Land of Turtles, 1999

lee LELA

Pat Gets a Prank Call, 1999
Ink on paper
20 x 25 cm / 8 x 10 in.

Statement

I drew this cartoon character by chance and I had no idea what I was doing. I guess it came from my inner anger of being made to feel like an outsider. Now people tell me that I am doing all these great things for women and women of color. I guess I am. But I'm really doing it because it makes me happy with myself and also because I wouldn't know how to do anything else.

78

Birthplace & year: Los Angeles, 1974
Grew up in a suburb of Los Angeles where her family was one of the very few Asians. The difference of her cultural heritage and physical features were made apparent and emphasized by schoolyard bullies. Her work Angry Little Girls revisits her angst-filled childhood and reclaims her past with humor and light.

Pat Gets a Prank Call, 1999

Maria- Have a Good Day, 1999
Ink on paper
20 x 25 cm / 8 x 10 in.

Kim sells Lemonade, 1999
Ink on paper
20 x 25 cm / 8 x 10 in.

Description

Angry Little Girls was expanded from her
cartoon character Angry Little Asian Girl which
was first a short video created while Lee was in
college. Three years later, she introduced her
heroine in five short episodes to the public. The
warm reception of the Angry Little Asian Girl led
Lee to expand her work to include other
characters evolving her short video into the
comic strip Angry Little Girls.

80

Kim sells Lemonade, 1999

Maria - Have a Good Day, 1999

lemoine MIHEE-NATHALIE painting, poetry

Young, 2001
Mixed media on rice paper
57.5 x 44.5 cm / 22.5 x 17.5 in.

Birthplace & year: Pusan, 1968
Multimedia artist and activist for adoptees' rights
(Search support and Visa).
Working in film, video, painting, and poetry.
Published internationally. Received grants from
the Brussels Multimedia Center and the University
of Wisconsin. Awarded at the Brussels Short Film
Festival, Seoul Documentary Film Festival and
sponsored by Eukorail, Royal Belgian Embassy,
Social Welfare Society, Agfa-Korea.
Has exhibited solo and group shows in Korea,
Taiwan, Hong-Kong, Germany, United States and
Canada.

Statement

I am interested in communication with foreign
sounds, meanings, and pronunciation.
Through culture, the connection with the
visual/graphic and interpretation will be
understood, misunderstood, or puzzled.

When the body doesn't fit the mind
When the language doesn't fit the person
When the race doesn't fit the language
When the mind doesn't fit the person

Young, 2001

Variation on Womyn, 2001
Mixed media on rice paper
12 x 30 x 30 cm / 12 x 12 x 12 in.

Suck Me-Ho's First English Lesson, 1999
Collage on paper,
21 x 29 cm / 8.5 x 11.5 in.

84

Description

My work has changed with places I have lived
and experiences I had been through, from
"pleasant" landscapes to more personal
themes, such as identity, reproduction, faces
and bodies. My own interpretation of what is
calligraphy evolved to conceptualize and
symbolize objects of daily life, but also to
represent sounds from one language to
another. One thing that remains is to be
different, the need to communicate and
understand with different standards. Creating
my own universe of mixed media from what I
learned from places, culture and places,
support and techniques are specifically chosen
to represent the code of my work.

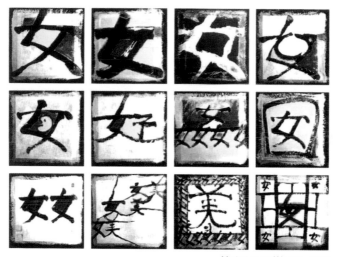

Variation on Womyn, 2001

INSTRUCTIONS. Study the following sentences. **Read and Repeat** the sentences again and again until you can recite them all from memory using correct **pronunciation, intonation** and **without looking at your book.** Practice substitution drills.

1. Let me <u>introduce myself</u>.

2. Allow me to introduce myself.

3. I'd like to introduce myself.

4. My name is **석, 이호** / I'm **Suck, Me-Ho**.

5. Please call me <u>Mr. **Suck**</u> / You can call me <u>Mr. **석**</u> / My friends call me "**Suck**".

6. <u>We haven't been introduced. My name is "**Suck**"....</u>
   Suck, Me-Ho.

7. I'm from Korea.

Suck Me-Ho's First English Lesson, 1999

Restruction, April 14th, 1999
Poem

Birthplace & year: Seoul, 1974
Overseas Adoptee, majored in Sociology/Asian
Studies at Michigan State University. Spent a
year in Korea teaching English in 2000. Work
has appeared in Detroit Metro Times. Featured
poet in forthcoming Seeds: Sisters of Color
Literary Journal. Published in Korean Quarterly.
Summer Writing Contest winner-Metro Times.
Editorial board for the Detroit chapter of a
national organization of Sisters of Color who
publishes SEEDS. Counselor for G.O.A.L.
(Global Overseas Adoptee Link).

Statement

Writing for me is about insight and discovery,
about opening up everything that has formed us
good or bad. I hope to inspire others to self-
reflect and challenge the limitations of our own
personalities and everyday realities and
influence others to take in the world with a fuller
awareness of the possibilities that exist in our
lives.

Description

My work is an attempt to share the many
whispers of an inner voice presented in a way
the reader can define themselves and society in
accordance to their way of the world. Most of
my pieces have a tone revealing whatever I
have confronted as a form of progression
drawing me to that full potential of
consciousness exploring how race/class/gender
intersect, how we filter our surroundings and
bringing light to a broader platform of the
multiple identities of Asian women.

Melting

Dripping
tears
like a candle crying

My sweatdrops
are
wax
rolling
forming
a
larger base

Some remain tall and fresh
Some trim
and
impatiently wait for new apple green leaves to start

Once the original
is lost
strength
is lost

Upshouts and spruts replace
but never replace the root
Left to grasp the saved hand full of air and pretend internal strength

Repeat trances to trace the misplaced
or
mend

But only shed more sweatdrops

Pealing Petals, 1999
Poem

Pealing Petals

Pealing
Petals of
Programming from mom and step-dad #3
that rum and coke on the freeway is OK.

Pealing
Petals of
Promises that mom and step-dad #4
will be back by the AM

Pealing
Petals of
Pretend lumps in my throat when my brother
escaped to the Navy leaving mom to start
brushing my hair and bathing me.

Pealing
Petals of
Pressure being mistaken in public as my dad's
mail-order picture bride.

Pealing
Petals of
Prototype passive, pleasing Geisha or
Masseuse eager to appease any AmeriKKKan man.

Pealing
Petals of
Propositions for paid passion from professors,
veterans and athletes.

Pealing
Petals of
Poking unprotected penises of fraternity boys
wanting 'hot ORIENTal chic's.'

Pealing
Petals of
Potential photo shoots for Playboy presenting
collegiate Oriental-gurls in 38-C

Pealing
Petals of
Potential risks on the east-side of town near the
1982 sLAUGHering of Vincent Chin.

Pealing
Petals of
Petty threats from my brothers to be replaced by
another GOOK if I didn't take a puff.

Pealing
Petals of
Profit for WHITE POWdER in plastic bags for dead presidents.

Pealing
Petals of
Pressure from family to marry a white-boy and
drive Fords, not 'rice burners.'

Pealing
Petals of
Personal victimization as an presumed
IMmiGRAnT at the border without a passport.

Pealing
Petals of
Puncture scars decorating my wrists like
bangles from failed suicide.

Pealing
Petals of
Pain and stems of static surfacing in my sleep
making my pulse pound.

Pealing
Petals of
Purging protein like plzza or peorgies into the
toilet hoping to vanish into THIN air.

Pealing
Petals of
Phlegm and sweat spidering down my 'flat
pancake' face waiting for my u-ma to return.

Pealing
Petals of
PROPAGANDA to ASSimilate and ADOPT
white western culture PERIOD.

II Planting rows of rice ready to become solid
and soak up all shades, sauces and spices.
Revealing my roots of brand new buds
blooming, breathing and being.

oh JI-YOUNG

The Wide Blue Yonder, 1998
Acrylic & fabric
193 x 122 cm / 76 x 48 in.

Statement

If I had to define my work in a short phrase, it would be "surreal dreams, chance, and reality in time." I face a blank white panel while feeling myself about to leap into the unreal world, yet with a sense of reality. The precious moment, a subtle body movement, unforgettable experiences from the past, the truth, and the unknown future, all become a visual form in my art.

90

Birthplace & year: Kwangju, 1964
Born in Kwangju, a city vibrant in art and culture. Began painting as a young child. Emigrated to the United States at the age of sixteen. Received a BFA at California State University Fullerton, and MFA from Claremont University. Incorporating non-traditional materials in innovative ways. Creates large works that are powerful and provocative. Exhibited globally.

The Wide Blue Yonder, 1998

My Pretty Rose Tree, 1996
Acrylic on panel
119.5 x 239 cm / 47 x 94 in.

Time for You, 1999
Graphite on paper
139.5 x 89 cm / 55 x 35 in.

92

Description

The vital and ambivalent meanings that I want to express operate through physically separated images, handled in different manners, and then metaphysically fused into one. It involves the combination of abstraction and realism of physical and emotional expression of human and his/her race. As of camera shutters simultaneously click at the different angles of an image, I combine images that connect in most imaginative way. If I could expand the size of what I know with my ability to visualize and reinstate it, I might see reality in wider perspective and hope that others would do the same. What is reality? That is my search right now.

My Pretty Rose Tree, 1996

Time for You, 1999

Pasta con fagioli, 1999
Acrylic on canvas
61x 45.5 cm / 24 x 18 in.

All my moving and traveling contribute to what and how I am. Wherever one is, I find all of us share the same thing in life. Love…which raises and answers many questions. Being born and raised partly in Seoul and my traveling experiences has shaped my life to always be ready for changes. The journey tends to be more spiritual than physical as I mature. Now I make paintings like simmering food for a long period of time, however, the food still must be cooked thoroughly. My search for the right food begins again in my mid-thirties.

94

Birthplace & year: Seoul, 1965
Born and raised in Seoul until age sixteen at which time went to study abroad. Chose the USA based on the American education system represented in mass media. By receiving education in two distinct cultural environments, way of thinking was opened greatly. After graduating from University of California, Irvine, studying art, lived in Italy to experience a different environment.
Currently lives in Los Angeles.

Pasta con fagioli, 1999

Coffee Break, 2000
Acrylic on canvas,
77.5 x 81 cm / 30.5 x 32 in.

Pasta I & II, 2000
Acrylic on canvas
91.5 x 91.5 cm / 36 x 36 in.

Description

My current work is about food. We are the
closest to food than anything else in our daily
lives. Babies automatically open their mouths
whenever food appears. We as humans, are
meant to be nurtured; making these images
was a different type of nutrition for me. My
exhibitions have gone appetizingly well on the
restaurant walls of LA.

96

Coffee break, 2000

Pasta I & II, 2000

pfenning JILL M.

Self-portrait, 1996
Plywood, plexiglass, various other media
244 x 122 x 183 cm / 8 x 4 x 6 ft.

I am most interested in the relationship that exists between people and the spaces that they use on a daily basis, and how that relationship can be expressed through the architecture of those spaces. I find that a lot of "modern" architecture and industrial design has produced very cold, lifeless buildings and interiors that do not address the complexity and specificity that makes individuals unique. I am interested in further exploring the ways in which architecture can address those spaces and the uniqueness which can come from this set of constraints.

Birthplace & year: Taegu, 1974
Born in Korea and adopted into a family in the United States at 15 months old. Grew up in a rural Vermont town of 3,000 people. Studied art and architecture at Wesleyan University in Middletown, Connecticut. Lived in Korea for a year teaching English through the Fulbright ETA Program in 1999-2000.

Self-portrait, 1996

Self-portrait, 1996
Plywood, plexiglass, various other media
244 x 122 x 183 cm / 8 x 4 x 6 ft.

Description

This work is entitled *Self-portrait*. It began as an investigation of small spaces, to answer the question, "how small of a space is still livable?" and evolved into an expression of the kind of space that I needed to be comfortable. Each detail in the construction (at full scale) expresses some personal need and the way that I met that need materially in keeping with the original goal of a small construction.

100

Self-portrait - inside view, 1996

Self-portrait - upper inside view, 1996

Homeless, 1996, Seoul
Performance

102

Birthplace & year: estimated Seoul, 1972
Adopted as a small infant and grew up in
Indianapolis, IN. While attending Wesleyan
University, began exploring adopted Korean
heritage through writing a literature honors
thesis and creating dance poetry performances.
Continued dance-poetry pieces on adoption in
Seoul and Yong-in, Korea and in communities of
adopted peoples in the United States. Finished
a Masters degree in Physiology, attending
medical school at Indiana University.

Statement

Dance and words help me to traverse between
seemingly disparate worlds; the United States
and Korea, my identities as a woman, Korean,
American, and the differing manifestations of
spirit: God, samshin, halmoni, Buddha. Dance
entered my life at the age of seven when I
entered my first ballet class. In college, I made
the transition to postmodern Western dance
and West African dance. Both dance styles -
the improvisational techniques and relationship
of movement and drumming, laid the foundation
for my shift into traditional Korean dance and
drumming after college. My poetry has been
my "pillow confessor" for my shifts and leaps
into self-understanding since I was in high
school.

Homeless, 1996

Secret Lives/Shared Lives, 1998, Yongin
Performance

Description

My dance/poetry/drumming performances have
been piecing together various parts of my
adoption narrative - my white American family
background and my unknown Korean heritage -
and represent a fusion of cultures. Dance and
words and drumming keep me integrated and
whole. The dance is ongoing; I myself am still
much "in progress."

104

Secret Lives / Shared Lives, 1997

41 Days, 2000
41 black & white silver photos with texts
124.5 x 124.5 cm / 49 x 49 in.

Statement

Like Asian Americans born in the United States, Asian Americans adoptees experience almost total immersion in American culture. But in a multi-cultural society increasingly concerned with developing one's pride in one's ethnic heritage, cross-cultural adoptees broken link to their past culture via ancestry and tradition sometimes creates a web of contradiction and confusion regarding identity. Some of my works explore the loss of ethnic culture and genetic links using grids to fragment my past; while others use grids to blend together family photographs which document the love and attention that I have received throughout my life.

106

Birthplace & year: Korea
Work has been exhibited nationally. Received the Carol Crow Memorial Fellowship, sponsored by the Houston Center for Photography under the auspices of 1999 Photography Fellowship program. Fellow in the 1995 New York University American Photography Institute's National Graduate Seminar. Received MFA in photography from Texas Woman's University in Denton, TX, and is currently the director of publications.

41 Days, 2000

Piecing Together Our Histories: A Korean
Adoptees Quilt, 1999
Cyantype, cotton muslin
178 x 152.5 cm / 70 x 60 in.

Description

*Piecing Together Our Histories: A Korean
Adoptees Quilt* was created to reflect the
experiences of Korean adoptees for the exhibit:
Snapshot: A Portrait of Korean Adoptees
at the Korean American Museum in Los
Angeles in 1999. Sponsler circulated an e-mail
request to Korean adoptees asking for their
photos and their thoughts about adoption.
Seventeen adoptees, including Sponsler, are
pictured on the quilt, which was commissioned
by the Association of Korean Adoptees -
Southern California, and the Korean American
Museum for the museum's permanent
collection.

108

Piecing Together Our Histories: A Korean Adoptees Quilt, 1999

Naked Eyes, Naked Soul: Hong Seok Cheon, 2000
Sepia-tone photo
25 x 20 cm / 10 x 8 in.

Statement

Traveling the world, facing different culture and finding our identity as a "human being" was always my quest. What makes us so unique, why we "meet" with someone and not with another? The line of our destiny with the multiple interactions we are facing in our everyday is an important part of my work.

110

Birthplace & year: Pusan, 1968
Adopted to a Belgian French family in Brussels, Belgium. After studying photography in Brussels, had several solo exhibitions and worked as a fashion photographer for fashion magazines in France & Belgium. Returned to Korea in 1995 to discover his birth culture. KameleonZ member and actively works as a fine art & fashion photographer.

Naked Eyes, Naked Soul: Hong Seok Cheon, 1999

The Light, 1999
Color print
50 x 40 cm / 20 x 16 in.

Angie Hsu, 2000
Polaroid
25 x 20 cm / 10 x 8 in.

112

Description

My eyes and soul were poured into each roll of
film used to immortalize images I saw as worthy
of recognition. It has been said that 'beauty is
in the eye of the beholder,' and I wanted to
show the world that the same is true for fame.
The people photographed here are all famous
to me and to them I have stripped myself
naked. My act of exhibitionism serves as a
symbol of my sincerity and dedication to true
artistic passion and expression. Nudity and
nakedness portray us as we truly are. I tried to
capture what clothing tries to hide from me.

The Light, 1999

Angie Hsu, 2000

Searching for Gohyang, 1998, USA
Documentary, color 16mm, Beta SP
31 min.

Statement

I want to tell stories in an honest and true way.
Whether it is about personal struggles, injustice
or the search for identity and belonging, I hope
each story will transcend beyond the individual
and bring a deeper reflection and awareness.

Birthplace & year: Korea, 1975
Attended Ithaca College on full scholarship,
majoring in Cinema & Photography. Searching
for Go-Hyang has been shown nationality at
festivals and on television. Won Best Non-
fiction film Award at Ithaca College and Best
Student Video at the New England Film and
Video Festival.
Currently lives in New York, works
independently in film and video.

Searching for Go-Hyang
A Film by Tammy Tolle (Chu Dong Soo)
Co-Produced by Una Kim
©1998 WaterLight Productions

Searching for Gohyang, 1998

Searching for Gohyang, 1998, USA
Documentary, color 16mm, Beta SP
31 min.

Description

Searching for Go-hyang (Homeland) is a
personal documentary exploring the
complexities of family ties, memories, identity,
and the search for a place of belonging. After
nearly fourteen years of separation, twin sisters
are reunited with their parents and two younger
brothers in Korea. What unfolds is a story of
what led the twins to be sent away. Distanced
by language and time, their only connection
with each other is their past and their
memories. The film also explores the
complexity of interracial/intercultural adoption,
and the family's difficulty is coming to terms with
the knowledge that an abusive white American
family had adopted the twins. It is about the
choices we are sometimes forced to make as
well as the contradictions and the reconciliation
in our lives.

116

Searching for Gohyang, 1998

Untitled (Puzzle), 1999
Wood blocks, black & white prints
28 x 28 cm / 11 X 11 in.

My work explores the complexities of being a member of an ethnic minority, a female, and a transracial adoptee. Like many other Korean adoptees, my experience is that of the outsider, even within the Asian American and Korean American Communities. To examine this perpetually marginalized state, I rely on oppositions such as the fragmented/hybrid, silence/speech, self-perception/stereotypes, and the persistence /absence of memories. Acknowledging the liminal space between such polarities allows for the shifting interplay between cultures and viewpoints, and establishes the greater possibility of being both/and rather than simply either/or.

118

Birthplace & year: Seoul, 1969
Adopted to United States at age five. Majored in French Literature at the University of Paris and in English Literature at the City College of New York. Is active in contemporary art as a writer, artist and curator. Was the Assistant Director at the NY Center for Media Arts, a groundbreaking new media art center with a focus on Korean artists.
Currently directing a documentary on international contemporary Korean artists for 2003 release.

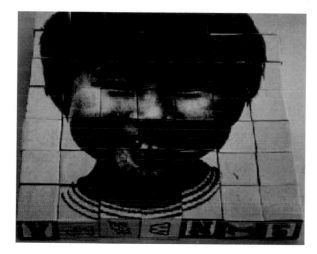

Untitled, 1999

Can't Put Humpry Together, 1999
Eggs & papernews in Hangul
Dimension variable

OMA / OVA (Year of the Rooster), 1999
Color prints
30.5 x 137 cm / 12 x 54 in.

Description

My technique is based in crafts such as sewing
and paper collage which, in their homeliness
and familiarity, facilitate the expression of these
unwieldy issues of identity.
In making visible my personal experience, I
hope to weave in universal questions of
existence, to strengthen the fabric of our shared
contemporary experience.

OMA / OVA (YEAR OF THE ROOSTER)
"Oma" is the Korean word for "mother," a primal
utterance homophonic with "ova," Latin for
"egg." I was born in 1969, the Year of the
Rooster. Each panel of the triptych is a syllabic
depiction:
"O" the wail of longing, the cry of pain or of
pleasure
"M" the suppressed or repressed, the withheld
or silenced
"A" the cry of birth, of relief, of repose
Language gives birth to a beginning and to a
sense of self. Motherless, through language we
become our own genitors.

Can't Put Humpty Together, 1999

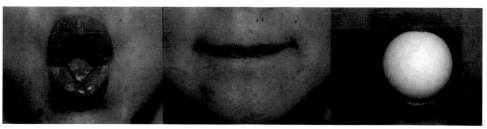

OMA /OVA (Year of the Rooster), 1999

group

Han Diaspora

KameleonZ

KimLeePark Productions

Tiger 2000

han DIASPORA

www.chomihee.com/handiaspora.html

Space for Shadows 96
Leah Sieck
Mihee-Nathalie Lemoine
Kim Myung-Bun
Ariko Ikehara

Space for Shadows 97
Me-K. Ahn
Mi Ok Song Bruining
Kate Hershiser
Susan Sponsler

124

Space for Shadows 98
Hijoo Son
Raymond Hahn
Kim Sungmin
Bamby Jones

Introduction

Han Diaspora, co-founded by Son Hijoo and Cho Mihee, in 1997, was created to provide an arena for reflection, debate, and discussion. The questions and inquiries which motivated their creation stem from the many contestations and discomforts within Korea.

Herein lies the phenomena: as the only divided nation in this post-Cold War era, and as the most homogeneous people, living more scattered throughout the world than within its own national boundaries, how are we to understand what being "Korean" means and/or what Korean citizenship means? This is the core question undergirding HD's existence, and we hope to challenge the Korean public to [re]think their understanding of the "Korean" identity and the context complicating this term. From this focus, there are many questions, issues, and dilemmas for debate and discussion.

Meaning: The term Diaspora as first coined in 1967 A.D. when the Jewish people were forced to leave their homeland by the Romans, leaving them displaced, thus creating a Diaspora. Han means Korea, One, In Between, Bright or Hopeful. Han Diaspora presented a multimedia artistic performances entitled, *Space for Shadows* (S4S) in Seoul, Korea during 3 consecutive years. They involved four artists each who were either adopted abroad, mixed race, Gyopo, or experienced life on a military base town.

KameleonZ

www.chomihee.com/kameleonz

Members
Ji Sun Sjogren
Mihee-Nathalie Lemoine
Choe Jooyoung
Byun Hyo In
Vincent Sung
Hyuna Park
Whang Bo-Ryung
Lee Sang Eun
Ines Cho
Johan
Ahn Jeong-Ae

Introduction

KameleonZ is a Korean-born multimedia artist group established since 1996, Seoul, co-founded by JiSun Sjogren and Cho Mihee

Along with these changes are the newly emerging groups of artists, among which not only deviant, but also female and non-Seoul artists, such as the adoptees, the second generation Koreans and Korean who studied abroad make up this trend. Art is viewed no longer linear in terms of particular school or sect, and more often than not the argument of artistic themes either "being international" has become the critical issue of discussion
Amid this cultural movement, the KameleonZ acts as a bridge between East and the West. KameleonZ seems to know how to sincerely approach that issue by sharing with the viewer their experiences and feelings on the subject of differences, and they strive to go beyond by learning the hard way, while working independently, what is to fraternize assimilate, and harmonize... i.e. to create and express their own unique culture.
'K' is a calligraphy to symbolize the influence of East has on our artistic endeavors.
The remainder of the word in Gothic lettering represents in turn our Western heritage.

125

KimLeePark PRODUCTIONS group

Introduction

KimLeePark Production is an Art and Action group established since 1999 and co-founded by Kim Bap, Lee Jung, Park Ki.

In order to address the needs of the Overseas Adoptee Korean(OAK) community, the Republic of Korea National Assembly sponsored a Human Rights Forum on adoption issues. April of 1998, at the Parliament Building located in Youido, Seoul, at least a hundred overseas Korean adoptees living in Korea, post adoption services, birth families, the media, and other interested Koreans attended the symposium. Here, adoptees Kim Han, Lee Jung, and Park Gi first met. Upon discussing their personal experiences as OAKs living in Korea, the three founded Kim Lee Park Productions (KLP), a group that uses art & action techniques to induce social change.

The Alien Awareness Project was introduced on Children's Day, May 5 of 1999. Eye-catching yellow stickers and masked aliens emerged on the streets of Seoul, along with *Re-Birth* a puppet performance that was presented at the Taehangno outdoor stage, seeking to raise the consciousness of the public of the Korean exiles situation. KLP joined efforts with KIN (Korean International Network), an organization that works for citizen rights, to gather over 1,000 signatures to approve the OAKs right to a special visa.

126

tiger 2000

Introduction

Committee for Korean Studies
Since 1998, Madison

The University of Wisconsin-Madison has
supported the curriculum on the cultures,
politics, languages and histories of China and
Japan. However, opportunities for teaching and
learning about Korea are almost non-
nonexistent on this campus.
1) To create Korea and Korean American-
related courses on this campus in the new
millenium for the benefit of all students and the
Madison community. It is our belief that the
University of Wisconsin Madison has the
potential to lead the development of this field in
Midwest.
2) To educate the University community about
Korea and Korean America--the complex
history, which has been in modern times
inextricably interwined with the United States,
and about Koreans in other global contexts.

The name of our committee, Tiger 2000, speaks
for our goal of establishing Korean/Korean
American studies by the turn of the millenium,
and we are committed to moving forward
with the energy of the tiger (horang-i)--a
powerful animal in Korean folk culture.

127

128

www.akava.org

The Archive of Korean American Visual Arts
Since 1999, California

Ahn, Young Il
Bae, Yoong
Bae, Jung Ran
Boed, Charlotte Kim
Chaa, Youn Woo
Choi, Soo
Han, Tsung Woo
Hwang, Sung Joon
Hyun, Hei Myung
Jhu, Michael
130 Kang, Kyung Ah
Kim, Ernie
Kim, Gee Won
Kim, Jung Sun
Lee, Ajean
Lee, Cecilia Hae-Jin
Lee, Yunsun
Lemoine, Mihee-Nathalie
Lew, Young June
Min, Helena JinAh
Oh, Ji-Young
Paik, Younhee
Park, Hye Ryon
Park, Hye Sook
Pickelle, John
Sponsler, Susan
Weimer, J. Maya

www.kaya.com

*Publisher of Asian/Diasporic Literature and Culture
Since 1994, New York*

*Kaya is dedicated to the publication of new and
innovative literature and the recovery of
important and often overlooked work from Asian
and the Asia diaspora.*

*Kaya's books range from individual volumes by
innovative poets and fiction writers to
comprehensive anthologies to its annual
publication of Asian diasporic culture and
society, MUAE.*

131

*In 1995, Kaya was awarded a Gregory
Kolovakos Seed Grant, sponsored by the
Council of Literary Magazines and Presses.*

*Kaya has been a sponsor of National Poetry
Month since 1997.*

www.koreamjournal.com

English Korean American Monthly Magazine
Since 1990, Gardena, CA
KoreAm's intent then and today is to provide
quality coverage on issues impacting the
community and to report on the achievements
of Korean descendants in America
KoreAm's mission statement is simple: to print
stories that touch upon the Korean American
experience. This embraces all generations,
including the mixed-race and adoptee
communities, and addresses a wide scope of
topics from business to politics, sports to
entertainment.

Past issues have covered the fallout of the
1992 L.A. Riots (in which more than 2,000
Korean-owned businesses were burned or
looted), the work of civil rights activist and
former Clinton appointee Angela E. Oh, the
struggles of the Korean American gay
community, comedian Margaret Cho and her
short-lived sitcom "All-American Girl," and
newer faces such as 1999 U.S. figure skating
silver medalist Naomi Nari Nam. After signing a
contract with Ingram Periodicals - the largest
magazine distribution company in the nation - in
May 1999, along with a number of smaller
distributors, KoreAm was made available in
select newsstands and bookstores in the U.S.,
Canada and Korea, including Borders and
Tower Records.

Introduction

Non-profit Korean-American Quarterly
Since 1997, Saint Paul, MN
Korean Quarterly is a non-profit quarterly
newspaper, written by and about the Korean
American community of the Twin Cities and
upper Midwest. We define this community to
include first and second generation Korean
Americans and their families (including non-
Korean family members), adopted Koreans and
their families, and bi-racial/bi-cultural Korean
American people.
We have a diverse Korean community in the
Twin Cities and the upper midwest. We come
from two cultures, several religions, and various
family backgrounds. But we have much in
common.
We treasure that part of us that identifies with
Korea and its people. We all want information
related to Korean American people and their
accomplishments, and we want to be kept
informed of the cultural, social and civic events
of the metro area Korean community.
Korean Quarterly offer a timely quarterly
newspaper in a lively feature format profiling
community leaders, role models, report
significant events, and chronicle the
accomplishments of our community's ordinary
people, both big and small. We list all Korean
religious, social, cultural and civic events which
are of interest to the community, including
events of interest to adoptees and their families.

134

West to East Exhibition

EVENSTILL Film Festival

Hello Kimchi Film Festival

KOREAMERICAKOREA Exhibition

west to east EXHIBITION

First Worldwide Korean Overseas Adoptee
Artists Exhibition
March 18-24, 1996
Samsung Insurance Gallery,Taejeon
Coordinated by YMCA-Taejeon & EKL-Korea
(Choe Young Mi and Cho Mihee)

Featured artists
Ji Sun Sjogren
Mihee-Nathalie Lemoine
Vincent Sung

136

Information

In the late Sixties or early Seventies, flights
from Korea to Europe used to go via Alaska
and the North Pole to finally reach, in our case,
Belgium. Today we can fly over the former
Soviet Union without being shot down. So
many things have happened in twenty-five
years one never reckoned possible. We first
generation of Korean-born European adoptees
have grown into adults. Nowadays we cannot
afford to think within the limits of national
frontiers. Today's industry and technology
enable if not forces us to think and act on a
global scale. In the field of art, we too have to
make those same efforts.
West to East is an exhibition that groups three
individual artists who have one thing in
common, cultural transmutation. In all others
respects the artists as different from one
another as flowers in a field.
We transcend all borders across the world
regarding our individual education and
upbringing. We also find ourselves in an
unique position where we can be both
Westerners and Asians at the same time.
This manifest itself in our different forms of
artistic expression and we would like to
challenge the Korean public to understand us in
this way as much as we try to understand our
birth country. Strange as it may sound, our
Koreanness binds us together in astounding
ways.

Korean Diaspora Film Festival
November 13-15, 1998
Minneapolis College of Arts & Design
Curator: Me-K. Ahn

List by chronological order:
Adoption - Mihee-Nathalie Lemoine,
1988, Belgium
Sally's beauty spot / Prey - Helen Lee
1990 / 1995, Canada
Through the milky way - Yun-ah Hong, 1992, USA
Great Girl, Kim Su Theller, 1993, USA
In memory to an identity - R. Vaughn, 1993, USA
Mama blues - Jae Soh, 1993, USA
My brown eyes - Jay Koh, 1994, USA
living in halftones / undertow - Me-k. Ahn
1994 / 1996, USA
Mr. Lee / Fighting Grandpa, Grey Park
1994 / 1998, USA
By the thinnest root / Kung Pao chicken - Richard Kim,
1995, USA
La senorita Lee - Hyn Mi Oh, 1995, USA
Yellow - Chris Chan Lee, 1996, USA
Looking for Wendy - Kimberly SaRee Tomes,
1997, USA
Crossing chasms - Jennifer Arndt, 1998, USA
Homes apart: Korea - Christine Choy and JT
Takagi, Korea

Information

EVENSTILL is an extra ordinary collection of work by Korean Adoptees and Gyopos (overseas Koreans) who share their experiences of living outside of Korea as foreigners, and as people who for political, economic and/or personal reasons, have left or were sent away from their motherland.

Three nights of documentary shorts, dramatic features, and experimental essays are paired together to expose the contradiction and confusion in 2 worlds-Korea & North America.

137

Programming assistance provided by Korean Overseas Adoptees (K.O.A-Seoul, Korea).

hello kimchi FILM FESTIVAL

Korean Overseas Film Festival
December 12-18, 1999
Dongsung Cinematheque, Seoul
Curator: Dongsung Art Center

Participants

Crickets - Jane E. Kim, Canada
Zoo - Radik Kim, Kazakstan
A Nursy Tale - Jie Ho Lee, USA
Buta no Mukui - Yang-Il Choi, Japan
Prey - Helen Lee, Canada
Knee High - Samuel Ha, USA
Mr. Black / Composed- Young mi Lee, England
By the Thinnest Root / Kung Pao Chicken -
Richard Kim, USA
Blue Chong - Sang Il Lee, Japan
45% Korean? - Mi hee Cho, Belgium
Annyong Kimchi - Matsue Tesuaki, Japan
Animal Appetites - Michael Cho, USA
Yun's Town - Woo-sun Kim, Japan
Mouse - Greg Park, USA
Disillusion - Yeong Hye Kim, England
Chinese Food and Donuts / Cowgirl - Sunny Lee,
USA
Yellow Bell - Chris Yoo, USA
Silent Broken - Kim Daeshil, USA
Nos traces silencieuses - Sophie Bredier and
Myriam Aziza, France
Bruno 34 years / Orson - Byun Hyuk, France
The Lover - Moon Seung-Wook, Poland
The Flight of the Bee - Biong Hun Min, Kazakstan

American-Korean Overseas Art Exhibition
May 27 - August 6, 2000
Art Sonje Center, Seoul

Participants
Byron Kim
Min Yunhee
Doho Suh
Sowon Kwon
Carole Kim
Soo Kim
Theresa Hak Kyung Cha
Michael Joo
Kyungmi Shin
Ikjoong Kang
Iara Lee

The title of this exhibition KOREAMERICAKOREA alludes to a process that has defined American experience since the country's birth. It conjures the idea of a convergence of different traditions to form both new nation and new culture. It is, to put it simply, a process of transformation and renewal. At any given moment in American history, one cultural tradition may have been predominant, but newer traditions are always in the making. In this exhibition, we see talented, creative people engaged in the process of building a new Korean American tradition. In so doing, there are, once again, transforming and renewing American culture.
(excerpts foreword by Christine Bosworth - Chairperson of the KOREAMERICAKOREA Steering Committee)

139

140

anthology

142

Introduction

Korean-American Anthology, 1992
Korean American Arts Festival Committee, CA
Editor: Paul Yi

Origin stories and contexts *Out of the ashes of Sa-i-gu*, the Korean American Arts Festival of 1992 emerged as a response to a widely felt need to share a grieving for the losses, but also to remember a living vitality and to dream a "politics of the possible." How could and how would Koreans speak to each other across demarcations of geography, gender, class, sexuality, language, and artistic media?

A newly (re)politicized group of individuals in the Korea/American community of the San Francisco-Oakland Bay Area began to put together an event that would provide a much-needed forum for Korean American artists to showcase their works.

Read individually and together, the submissions evoked for me a range of memories, feelings, and new perspectives. But the overwhelming response that many pieces produced in their reading was an uncanny sense of familiarity (by Kang Hyun Yi, 1994, Oakland)

muae

MUAE 1: Premier Issue
Edited by Walter K. Lew
The inaugural volume features art and writing by
Yi Sang, Kang Nae-hui on Lotte World's shaping
of consumer experience in Seoul, paintings on
military sex slavery by Miran Kim, photographs
on scale and simulacra at Florida's Splendid
China by Richard Barnes, and scenes from Nam
June Paik's Tribute to Charlotte Moorman.

MUAE 2: Collapsing New Buildings
Edited by Lawrence Chua
MUAE 2 looks at the ways development has
been theorized in an Asian context and
interrogate the ways historical ideas of progress
have been considered. To facilitate the
exchange of critical ideas among diasporic and
Asian communities, a third of Collapsing New
Buildings has been translated into Korean.

MUAE 3: Contagion
Edited by Lawrence Chua
Coming this winter!

Introduction

Annual Series of Anthologies on Transcultural
Production, since 1995

"MUAE...[goes] beyond simple attempts to
elevate the 'outsider' and challenge[s]
assumptions about the individual's relations to
his or her culture.... The works...are of such
high quality and unique voice as to cast light
and shadows on each other while standing
separately."
--Library Journal, "The Best Magazines of 1995"

A startling remix of innovative creative writing,
controversial dialogues, provocative artwork,
and investigative journalism, MUAE is Kaya's
annual publication of Asian and Asian diasporic
culture and society. "Muae" literally means
"without hindrance"--a Korean Buddhist term
that describes the interdependent relationship
of all things, where every entity and event
becomes enmeshed in an open net of
transcultural collaboration, conflict, shifts, and
reflection.

143

seeds FROM A SILENT TREE

144

Introduction

Korean Overseas Adoptee Anthology, 1997
Publisher: Pandal Press, CA
Editors: Jo Rankin & Tonya Bishoff

Seeds from a Silent Tree explores the embodiment of both and neither. In the spirit of the origin of the anthology [from the Greek anthos, flower + legein, gather], both professional and novice writers gather here to explore the complexities intertwined in transracial adoption. Through poetry, fiction and personal narratives, Korean adoptees speak in their own voices, struggling to negotiate an individual space that fluctuates according to their soil, environment, and nourishment - emotional, physical, spiritual.

With this anthology, we seek to break a certain silence - silence from our land of origin, silence from the lands we now inhabit - tongues tied by racism, some external, some painful internal; tongues tied by social mores, codes, and contradictions; tongues tied by colonialism myths of rescue missions and smooth assimilation.

Introduction

Collection of Works from a Generation of Overseas
Korean-born Adoptees, 1999
Publisher: Young & Young, MN
Editor: Susan Soon-Keum Cox

In deepest recesses of memory, perhaps some
clue remains, some shadowy recollection of a
mother, of a land, now foreign, yet somehow
vaguely familiar.

They began life in Korea, but circumstances
took them thousands of miles away to adoptive
families in America, Europe and Australia.
From childhood they grew into their adopted
cultures, but the reflection in the mirror, the
whispers of strangers and the quiet beating of
the heart perhaps told them of another land...
seen through the eyes of a small child, felt in
the language of a child's heart.

The writings and works contained in this book
reflect experiences of Korean adoptees. They
are images and words that can never be
completely removed from that child in Korea.
They are *Voices from Another Place.*

145

annexes

contacts

Me-K Ahn
ando@mtn.org
ww.utensil.net/ahn
11516 Ravoux Ave, Minneapolis, MN 55337, USA

Michou Amelynck
michou.a@advalvas.be
Avenue de l'Arbre Ballon, 137 B-1020 Bruxelles,
Belgium

Charlotte Kim Boed
ckboed@hotmail.com
www.ckboed.dk
Oestbanegade 39 2tv 2100 Copenhagen,
Denmark (Tel. +45 3538 3398)

Jiwon Chun
jiwonchun@yahoo.com
USA

Kimberly Kaye Nam Il Dalros
kkdalros@hotmail.com
194 Summit Ave. #202, St. Paul, MN 55102, USA
(Tel: +1 651 225 4749)

Meaghan Dunn & Kevin Kahiler
uijung@slip.net, kkahiler@mediaone.net
www.kittybobo.com
USA

JeeYun Ha
jeeyunha@hotmail.com
241 Valley Road, Wayne, NJ 07470 USA

Raymond Hahn
cajuboy@yahoo.com
C. PO Box 3480, Seoul 100-634, Korea
(Tel: +82 16-682 1747)

Zoli Kim Hall
zolihall@uswest.net
www.zolihall.com
USA

Stephanie Han
buddhafun@aol.com
www.stephaniehan.com
USA

Kate Hers
kate@onegook.com
www.onegook.com
K. P.O. Box 465, Seoul 110-604, Korea
(USA Voice Message: +1 810 468 1827)

Song Huff
mothsup@yahoo.com
USA
(Tel: +1 646.246.6308)

Meejah I-Ley
l-ley@usa.net
Seoul, Korea

148

contacts

Jung
jung@swing.be
www.eurobd.com/jung
Brussels, Belgium

Jean Jung
jeanjung@hotmail.com
1177 Academy Drive, Youngstown, OH 44505, USA

Min Jung Kim
Email: minjung@iistix.com
Website: www.minjungkim.org
2073 Magellan Drive, Oakland, CA 94611, USA

Cecilia H. Lee
fluxmaster@aol.com
www.nakedrabbit.com/haejin/
Box 36673, Los Angeles, CA 90036, USA
(Tel: +1 323 913 1210)

Lela Lee
alag@angrylittleasiangirl.com
www.angrylittlegirls.com
Gorilla Productions
P.O. Box 241576, Los Angeles, CA 90024, USA

Mihee-Nathalie Lemoine
chomihee@hotmail.com
www.chomihee.com
K. P.O. Box 1964, Seoul 110-619, Korea

Yun Sook Kim Navarre
seoulflower@yahoo.com
www.chomihee.com/navarre
Detroit, USA

Ji Young Oh
jioh@gte.net
21433 Ambushers St., Diamond Bar, CA 91765,
USA (Studio: +1 909 595 6125)

Hyuna Park
hyunapark@hotmail.com
1979 Grace Ave #3A, Los Angeles, CA 90068, USA
(Tel: +1 323 850 6622)

Jill M. Pfenning
jillpfenning@yahoo.com
2202 Brand Farm Drive, South Burlington, VT 05403, USA

Leah Sieck
lsieck@iupui.edu
314 N Audobon Rd., Indianapolis, IN 46219, USA
(Tel: +1 317 356 9963)

Susan Sponsler
s_sponsler@TWU.edu
www.twu.edu/~s_sponsler/
Office of Public Information, Texas Woman's University
P.O. Box 425619, Denton TX 76204, USA
(Tel: +1 940 898 3454)

149

contacts

Vincent SUNG
seoulfashion@yahoo.com
www.modelplus.net/photo/photographers/vincent/
photo_works_set.html
Seoul, Korea

Tammy Tolle
dongsoo8@aol.com
23-36 31st Ave. #2R, Astoria, NY 11106, USA

J. Maya Weimer
mayaweimer@hotmail.com
NYC, USA

Eleanor Soo-Ah HYUN
eshyun@hotmail.com
NYC, USA

KameleonZ
hyunapark@hotmail.com
K. P.O. Box 1964, Seoul 110-619, Korea

Han Diaspora
hijoo_son@yahoo.com

KimLeePark Production
K. P.O. 465, Seoul 110- 604, Korea

Tiger 2000 - Committee for Korean Studies
University of Wisconsin-Madison
239 "The Old Red Gym"
716 Langdon St., Madison, WI 53706, USA

150

The following have supported the OKAY Book
with their generous contributions:

Asian American Arts Alliance
www.aaartsalliance.org

Matthew DOLBOW
Seoul, Korea

Peter Joon HAN
NYC, USA

Henry R. HAGGARD
US Embassy, Seoul

Haesong Child Wefare Society
Tel.: +82 2 720 5251
koreanid@kornet.net

IL Arts Council, Chicago
www.stateil.us/agency

JinSolBooks
www.jinsolbooks.com
Seoul, Korea

Korean Street Festival Chicago
Aug. 11-12, 2001
Tel: +1 773-583-1700

Lady Fest Midwest
www.ladyfestmidwest.org

NAATA, San Francisco
National **A**sian **A**merican
Telecommunications **A**ssociation
www.naatanet.org

Old Town School of Music
www.oldtownschool.org
Royal Belgium Embassy
Seoul, Korea
www.belgium.or.kr

Royal Danish Embassy, Seoul
Tel.: +82 2 795 4187 Fax: +82 2 2 796 0986

151

The Sejong Cultural Outreach
www.sejong.linkage.org
E-mail:lgelbber@msn.com

The Witch's Table
+82 2 732 27 27

Me-k Ahn	living in haltones, undertow
Michou AMELYNCK	Chemim de L'Anabiose, Here and Near
Charlotte Kim BOED	Moods of Silver, Identities
Jiwon CHUN	Our Home, Rubbing, Blue sponge
Kimberly Kaye Nam-Il DALROS	Balance, Landcape
Meaghan DUNN & Kevin KAHILER	Don't be Latte
JeeYun HA	Falling, Burning Bush, Shouldn't Touch
Raymond HAHN	Crossing My Own Pacific Ocean, The ID Line
Zoli Kim HALL	For Omoni, For Omoni-Part II
Stephanie HAN	Pale Yellow Moon, To Kill Is Desire
Kate HERS	My Country 'Tis of Thee, Sexy Girlfriend, American Milk
Song HUFF	Popular, Will Power, Asian Baby, Untitled
JUNG	Jeune Fille et le Vent
Meejah I-LEY	war, stranded
Jean JUNG	Untitled
Minjung KIM	Missed Flight, Restless, Brick
Cecilia H. LEE	Medicine Balls, Land of Turtles, Folktale Frogs
Lela LEE	Kim Sells Lemonade, Pat Gets a Prank Call, Maria-Have a Good Day
Mihee-Nathalie LEMOINE	Young, Variation on Womyn, Suck Me-Ho's First English Lesson
Yun Sook Kim NAVARRE	Restruction, Pealing Petals
Ji-Young OH	The Wide Blue Yonder, My Pretty Rose Tree, Time for You
Hyuna PARK	Pasta con Fagioli, Coffee Break, Pasta I & II
Jill M. PFENNING	Self-portrait
Leah SIECK	Secret Lives/Shared Lives, Homeless
Susan SPONSLER	41 Days, Piecing Our Histories
Vincent SUNG	Naked Eyes, Naked Soul, Angie Hsu, The Light
Tammy TOLLE	Searching for Go-Hyang
J. Maya WEIMER	Untitled, Oma/Ova, Can't Put Humpry Together
Hio-Kyeng LEE	Homeless
Jayleen SUN	L.A book cover design
Scott SCHRAEDER	L.A's book cover illustration

152

thanks

The coordinators would like to especially thank the following people who have given us much support and belief in our artistic endeavors.

AHN Sang-Joon (St. Ex)
Consul Sven BJODSTRUP (Royal Danish Embassy)
Jim CHOI (NAATA)
Kim DALROS
Matthew DOLBOW
Lindy GELBER (Camp Sejong)
Henry R. HAGGARD, The US Embassy
Eleanor Soo-Ah HYUN
Ellen Eun-Yang JIN (The Witch's Table)
Chris Jang (Korean Street Festival, Chicago)
Benjamin JOINEAU (St. Ex)
Todd D. KWAPISZ (Holt International)
LEE Eun-Jeong (Agfa Korea Ltd.)
LEE Hung-Yull (Adobe Systems Korea Ltd.)
LEE How-Uk (Adobe Systems Korea Ltd.)
LEE Eun-Wook (Yuhan-Kimberly)
LEE Misun (Social Welfare Society)
Bret MANTYK
Dr. Inoun PARK (Haesong Child Welfare Society)
PARK Jin-Deok (JinsolBooks Co.)
Dr. PARK Won-Kyun (Meeka Dental Clinic)
PARK Young-Sook (Agfa Korea Ltd.)
Ambassador Koenraad ROUVROY (Belgium Embassy)
Martha VICKERY (Korean Quarterly)
Chris WINSTON (K.A.A.N)
Stephen WUNROW (Korean Quarterly)

153

M E E K A
Dental Clinic

English - Francais
available

Dr. PARK W.K.

D.M.D., M.S.D., Orthodontist

02 - 3437 3335

parkwonkyun@hotmail.com

Location
Kui Subway Station (Green Line)
Exit 4 - ShinHan Bank (3 FL.)

F r e n c h
Wine Bar & Bistro

Le Saint-Ex

Tel/Fax (822) 795 2465

lesaintex@hotmail.com

Yongsan-Ku, Itaewon Dong 119-28
Seoul, Korea

Itaewon Subway Station 6th Line
(Parking available - Boo-Yeong Joocha-jang)

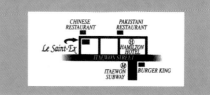

155

ARTIST INDEX BY COUNTRY

ARTIST INDEX BY DISCIPLINE